Seiz~~~~y

M000187958

Favourite Inspirational Poems
By Wayne Visser

Third Edition

Third paperback edition published in 2016 by
Kaleidoscope Futures, London, UK.

First paperback edition published in 2010 by
Your P.O.D. Ltd and second paperback edition
published in 2012 by Wayne Visser. First and
second electronic editions published in 2011 by
Wayne Visser and in 2016 by Kaleidoscope
Futures.

Cover photography and design by Wayne Visser.
Cover photograph of the author by Indira
Kartallozi.

Printing and distribution by Lulu.com.

ISBN 978-0-9570817-6-5

Dedication

To my muse in all her guises:

my raiment –
       cloaked in nature
       naked in passion
       silent in mystery
       bubbling in spirit
my wellspring –
       dark in gestation
       bright in revelation
       spitting in anger
       cooing in love
my instrument –
       shuddering in despair
       stretched in hope
       wailing in sadness
       resounding in joy
my visage –
       bashful in some ways
       boastful in others
       whispering in the night
       singing in the day
my companion –
       often away
       but never far
       never gone
       forever

Fiction Books by Wayne Visser

I Am An African: Favourite Africa Poems

Wishing Leaves: Favourite Nature Poems

Seize the Day: Favourite Inspirational
Poems

String, Donuts, Bubbles and Me: Favourite
Philosophical Poems

African Dream: Inspiring Words & Images
from the Luminous Continent

Icarus: Favourite Love Poems

Life in Transit: Favourite Travel & Tribute
Poems

Non-fiction Books by Wayne Visser

Beyond Reasonable Greed

South Africa: Reasons to Believe

Corporate Citizenship in Africa

Business Frontiers

The A to Z of Corporate Social
Responsibility

Making A Difference

Landmarks for Sustainability

The Top 50 Sustainability Books

The World Guide to CSR

The Age of Responsibility

The Quest for Sustainable Business

Corporate Sustainability & Responsibility

CSR 2.0

Disrupting the Future

This is Tomorrow

Sustainable Frontiers

The CSR International Research
  Compendium

The World Guide to Sustainable Enterprise

About the Author

Wayne Visser was born in Zimbabwe and has lived most of his life in South Africa and the UK. He is a writer, academic, social entrepreneur, professional speaker and amateur artist.

Wayne finds inspiration in all of life, nature and relationships, which is given voice through this collection. His views on inspiration are best summed up in his own words:

For me, to live is to create
To give expression, form and shape
To mould the forces, though unseen
To make and break, to shift and screen
To build with blocks of mind and soul
To learn and grow, to reach that goal
Life is neither chance nor fate
For me, to live is to create

Website: www.waynevisser.com

Email: wayne@waynevisser.com

Contents

Seize the Day

Sages through the ages wisely say:
Carpe Diem – seize the dawning day!
Oh, would that I could assuage that thirst
But the day conspires to seize me first!

With the hurry and scurry
Of home's frantic flurry
And the hustle and bustle
Of work's tangled tussle

With the knocks and blocks
Of life's surprise shocks
And the names and games
Of love's fickle flames

Alas! It's not the day that I seize
But the feathers floating in the breeze
And the jetsam drifting on the tide
That I cling to for my daily ride.

Mind-Seeds

I write my dreams in wisps of smoke
That swirl before the dawn;
And when I wake, my mind unblurs
To trace the edge of morn.

I rise with words, like tousled hair,
Still wild and unrestrained;
And when I brush them into place,
They fight to stay untamed.

Once at the gym, to treadmill beat,
Thoughts form and fall in line;
And when I stroke the cool blue lengths
The words swim laps in time.

Returning home, under the shower,
I write in jets of steam;
And after breakfast, at my desk,
I face a blinking screen.

I type one word – a secret key
Which opens many doors –
And gaze upon a sea of words:
An ocean spanning shores.

I dive into the frothy tides
With flailing, keyboard strokes;
And when I've splashed and made some
    waves,
Seek land before I choke.

I write day-dreams in digi-chrome
That spreads like inks that spill;
And when dusk falls, I find my words
Have travelled where they will.

I write my life in daily prose
That walks a winding road;
And as I write, my story springs
From mind-seeds I have sowed.

A Splash of Colour

A splash of colour in a sky
Which otherwise was grey
I met, above clouds on high
An artist on that day

On homeward flight, from my cocoon
Spun of corporate tire
She seemed to me a butterfly
With wings of bright desire

How was it that we spoke so free
On subjects so diverse?
As if upon a stage we played
Our dialogue rehearsed

For her, a brush, for me, a pen
Are keys to hidden doors
Behind which, upon eagle wings
Passion swirls and soars.

Step Out

Step out into the breaking day:
Step lightly and step brightly;
As best you can, step rightly
Upon your chosen way –
Step out into the breaking day.

Step out into the spritely Spring:
A-thudding and a-budding,
With colours all a-flooding
And joy upon a wing –
Step out into the spritely Spring.

Step out under the glaring sun:
Beyond the shade of sheltered glade
Into the forge where hearts are made
And life's true race is run –
Step out into the glaring sun.

Step out into the burning fire:
With dancing feet on blazing heat,

Defy the odds of self defeat
Through naked flamed desire –
Step out into the burning fire.

Step out into the gaping breach:
The bridge of sighs and stream of lies,
To stand astride the great divides
And stretch beyond your reach –
Step out into the gaping breach.

Step out into the fading Fall:
A-swirling and a-twirling,
Upon the breeze a-curling;
Responding to the call –
Step out into the fading Fall.

Step out into the sleet and snow:
It's dripping and it's slipping,
So walk with extra gripping;
Be careful as you go –
Step out into the sleet and snow.

Step out onto the fragile ice:
Cross hairline cracks and bear line tracks,
With quaking confidence that lacks
While fate is rolling dice –
Step out onto the fragile ice.

Step out under the gleaming moon:
While yearning tides and turning rides
Keep secrets that the future hides
Of lovers' lilting tune –
Step out beneath the gleaming moon.

Step out into the starlit night:
Step surely and step purely;
Take care, yet not demurely,
Upon your homeward flight –
Step out into the starlit night.

Sweet Seduction

Ah, the lure of books
Such sweet seduction!

The gentle curves
of a swaying body of words
The tasteful fabric
of an exquisitely draped cover
The alluring glint
in the eyes of an enigmatic character
The finely applied make-up
of colour-textured illustrations
The possessive dance
of an evolving rhythmic narrative
The aesthetic beauty
of a pose of inflective phrase

At the caress of literature
All resistance crumbles!

The Abyss

When you feel like you are falling
Into a gaping abyss
Endlessly, helplessly falling
Into a bottomless pit
Hold on tight
To your inner light
And count your starlit blessings
Don't ask why
Look up at the sky
And spread your radiant mind-wings

When you feel like you're depleted
Without an ounce of drive
Totally, utterly depleted
Without the will to strive
Light a fire
Of your heart's desire
And feed the flame with passion
Start a dream
Of a world unseen

And build it without ration

When you feel like you are alone
In a cruel uncaring place
Heartlessly, hopelessly alone
In a cold and empty space
Reach out and
A supportive hand
Will be right there above you
Share your fears
Your anger and tears
With those who really love you.

Horrendus Camena

Now listen to my rhyme –
A literary crime
About which may be said:
"It's something all should dread!"

For it stumbles its beat
And it fumbles its feet,
Faking phrases and words
Left free-floating like turds;
Plus the lines are all fraught
With ideas come to naught …

Oh, I'm filled with regret –
I just want to forget
Ever starting this lilt
That was destined to wilt …

Mine's the ultimate gaffe –
A dud-poem that's naff!

Peek-A-Boo

Blind looking without seeing –
Then a glimpse ...
Deaf listening without hearing –
Then a sound ...
Numb sensing without feeling –
Then a prick ...
Dumb speaking without saying –
Then a laugh ...

I see her peeking from among the clouds
Hear her softly whispering upon the breeze
Feel her gently tugging at my hair
Greet her gladly with affirming "yes".

She comes at the beckon of my indifference
Nods in empathy with my dissatisfaction
Frowns under the swirl of my confusion
Tempts me with a winked promise of
        rejuvenation

She has heard the mulled monotony
Of professional mantras chanted
Tasted the bland boredom
Of pedalled ideas regurgitated
Felt the tired treadmill
Of plodding paths travelled
Seen the smiling crack
In the grey shell-trap of routine

I see you - sparkling!
I hear you - fizzing!
I feel you - bubbling!
I greet you - bursting!
You scatter new seeds
Sprinkle magic dust
Trickle liquid energy
Shower nourishing rays

You bring the gift of yeast
Fermenting with expectation
Inside the needy dough
Of my daily bread

You are welcome
My familiar friend
Back to rescue me
Just in time
From un-caring.

Rainbow Beads

Your life is strung with sacred strings
Of shining, rainbow beads
Each capturing in brilliant ray
Your shimmering thoughts and deeds

You are the weaver of great skill
But cannot craft alone
The patterns hail from hidden source
The colours are home-grown

Each glistening bead becomes a gift
Upon the trail of life
And looking back, your path is strewn
With sparkling gems of light

This masterpiece of joy and strife
This quilt without mistake
Is ever-changing, never-ending -
A meaning-filled mosaic

So hold your beads up to the sun
Let inspiration shine
And thread your dreams upon the web
Of Spirit's grand design.

Catch Me If You Can

I've been released into the wild
Just like a wide-eyed, wondrous child
And though I travel far from home
I know I'll seldom be alone

I'm making friends along the way
And teaching adults how to play
I'm bringing unexpected joys
To lots of little girls and boys

To some, I am a mystery
To others, like a fantasy
I bring cold thrills and warm romance
But is it fate or is it chance?

So catch me if you can today
Tomorrow I'll be miles away
Or maybe just around the block
Or in your favourite coffee shop

And if you find me, pick me up
I'll share my life and bring you luck
Then set me free to make more friends
So that my story never ends.

Author's note: This poem is about the
delightful phenomenon of bookcrossing
– see http://www.bookcrossing.com

Look Up!

When you're feeling brown
Look up, not down
Don't fret or frown
Don't dig a hole
Don't be a mole
There's nothing much that's up
When you are underground
Instead, the thing I've found
Is that if I build a mound
I'm already much more such more up
Than ever I was down

And if you're feeling sad
It's not so bad
So don't get mad
Rather think of all the good things
Like chocolate books and magic rings
And flying without feathered wings
Or think of something really fun
Like playing in the sparkly sun

And belly laughing with someone
Or anything makes you glad
Just not what makes you sad

And if you're feeling low
Don't stop, just go
Go fast, not slow
Go with the flow
Or plant a seed of happy thoughts
And watch it sprout and grow
Then climb your wavy happy tree
And from the top you'll see, you'll see
You'll almost touch the sky
And when you are so high, you'll know
That you're no longer low

So when your sky is cloudy
Be bright, not dowdy
In fact be downright rowdy
Jump and dance and scream and shout
Don't keep it in, just let it out
And if you're loud and clear

The sun might even hear
And come out from its hiding place
And show its warm bright shining face
And say to you a sunny "Howdy ...
Look up! It's clear not cloudy".

The Artist's Gift

It was the faces
That first made me stop
And look
And linger

Their wise wrinkles
And smiling eyes
So alive
So beautifully African

How long had I searched
For carvings such as these
That reach into my heart
And whisper to my soul?

But the gift
That I thought I had found
Was not the gift
That I left with that day

It would have been easy
To dismiss him
As just another street trader
One of life's desperados

He had the look –
This scruffy Rastafarian
With lopsided grin –
Of the joker in the pack

But something about him
(Was it his manner?)
Drew me in closer
And made me take note

He told me his name
And oh so gently
He told me the story
Of his artist's life

It was clear to me
That he lived only to give life

To pregnant meanings
Forever gestating in his being

He showed me his drawings
Which swirled on music
And danced with contrast
And sang in symbols

And as he decoded each sign
And unlocked each emotion
Art became transformed
Into philosophy

Even the negotiation on price
(As if aesthetics can ever be valued)
Revealed layers of sensitivity
To deeper principles

For he spoke sincerely
Of the importance of finding balance
Between giving and taking
And having and being

Under the African sun
On the city pavement that day
I felt a connection that transcended
The suit and the T-shirt

And as I said farewell
Like old friends parting
For once in my life I had the courage
To speak my truth

"The money I gave
Is merely a token of my appreciation
For these priceless expressions
Of your artistic talents"

But more than this
You have my admiration and respect
For you have given me a much greater gift
Which is inspiration and insight"

Now whenever I look
At the wise old face

Carved in rough wood
I think of him

And I smile
And wish him every good fortune
Knowing that I am forever enriched
By the artist's gift

Fragments

You make impressions with canvass and
    paint
Weaving great stories of sunlight and shade
While I am a pilgrim with wonder and faith
Picking up pebbles of beauty and bliss

You cast silhouettes with chisel and stone
Freeing trapped figures of memoir and myth
While I am a pirate with word-sword and
    page
Hunting for treasures of wisdom and wit

You craft harmonies with lyric and beat
Riding vast oceans of motion and mood
While I am a healer with metre and rhyme
Tending to ailments of passion and pain

You spawn adventures with heroes and fate
Mapping new fusions of player and plot

While I am a shaman with sound-spells and
    dreams
Grasping at whispers of longing and love.

Born to Fly

Threads of words across the miles
Dyed with tears and strung with smiles
Ropes of friendship woven tight
Bridge the gulf of day and night

Splashes of smiles upon the page
Brushed with youth and coloured with age
Canvass of memories and imagination
Reveal the art of co-creation

Glitter of laughter sparkling bright
Eases the dark and catches the light
Circus of clowns who entertain
Shine joy to lift the clouds of rain

Feathers of touch against the skin
Caress without and tickle within
Flutter of wings across the sky
Reminds us that we're born to fly.

Book Lovers

So what if it's true
I sleep with my books
There's no need for you
To give me strange looks
It's just when I'm weary
From every day strain
I want my books near me
To massage my brain
It's a way to unwind
And let my thoughts go
It's relaxing I find
To let the words flow
Is that so insane?

So what if I keep
The dictionary next
To me when I sleep
So I don't get vexed
It's just when I'm dreaming
And wake up with words

Like bright ribbons streaming
And songs of the birds
It's best that I check them
To see if they fit
Rather than wreck them
Before they are writ
Is that so absurd?

So what if the sheets
I have on my bed
Are blank paper sheaves
To lay down my head
It's just when I wake up
With some swirling rhyme
Like leaves left to rake up
From star scattered time
It's better to scribble
The words on a page
And capture its riddle
Before the spark fades
Is that such a crime?

The Tunnel

Every tunnel has its ending
Every aperture its light
Every rainbow arch that's bending
Shows that you can win the fight

And though the tunnel may be black
And hardship cannot be denied
Keep moving forward, never back
And you will reach the other side

And as you sojourn in the dark
You have a secret light, it's true:
On every journey you embark
Your loved ones always ride with you.

Pictures and Words

A picture paints a thousand words
And sometimes words are not enough
For pictures go where words cannot follow
And words remain long after pictures fade

Pictures are doors to time travel
And words are windows on deep space
Together they map our world of dreaming
And bend perceptions of reality

Pictures capture what can be seen
And words release what was hidden
For pictures are creations of the light
And words are born in the womb of
    darkness

Pictures are freeze frames of history
And words are visions of the future
For pictures trap moments in glaciers
And words flow like rivers to the ocean

Pictures are mirrors of beauty
And words are tides of feeling
For pictures shine with colours of the sun
And words reflect the mood swings of the
moon

A word spells a thousand pictures
And sometimes pictures are too few
For words weave the stories of our lifetime
And pictures are cairns along the journey

Sky Dream

A moon beam to brush your cheek
A star burst to lift your eyes
A sun ray to touch your lips
A bird song to greet your rise

A wind gust to clear your head
A cloud wisp to thread your sighs
A rain drop to quench your heart
A snow flake to soothe your cries

A rose bud to kiss your nose
A tree top to bless your highs
A duck pond to cast your wish
A sky dream to loose your ties

Be My Kite

Be my kite:
Rise up from the earth
On a breath and a whisper
Dazzle in the sunshine
And tiptoe on the wind
Be brilliant in your beauty
And agile in your ability
Boldly fly your true colours
For your own delight
And for mine

Dart and duck and dive
As you streak across the blue
Leaving a ribbon trail
Swirl and shake and shimmy
As you sparkle in the light
Burning like a comet
Flash and flirt and flutter
As you perform your moves

For cheering terrestrials
And for me

Be my kite:
Stretch for your freedom
Beyond the ties that bind you
Feel the wind's desire
And the tug of remote intention
(Almost imperceptible)
Sail the rough sky-seas
Until you are all spent
Until you are ready
Ready to return

Fly for the joy of flying
Yet also for the pleasure of another
For without its flyer
A kite is like a tumbleweed
On a dusty track to nowhere
And strain against your leash
Yet not so hard that the bond snaps
For without its strings

A kite is like a leaf in autumn
At the wind's random mercy

Be my kite:
Resist the steady pull
Holding you back from the sun
Until you feel the warm glow
Of pulsing exhilaration
And hard-earned exhaustion
Then submit to the safety
Of the solid ground below
To be gently caressed
By rough hands

Reach for the horizon
Yet do not fear being grounded
For just as there is passion in wildness
So too is there satisfaction in peace
And in non-striving
Push out the boundaries
Yet do not fear known places either
For while there is tension in resistance

There is also relief in submission
And in letting-be

Be my kite:
Test your limits
But also trust the signals
Of the one who keeps you aloft
For to fly without strings
Is to soar free and high
But only for a fleeting moment
Before you plummet and crash
Perhaps never to rise
And fly again

Keep asking questions
And listen for the answers
For your strength is your awareness
Your sensitivity to subtle signs
And gentle shifts
Keep an open mind
And do not jump to conclusions
For your weakness is your stubbornness

Your failure to read the wind's moods
And trust the flyer's skills

Be my kite:
And follow your instincts
For you were born to fly
To dance across the sky
Moving to the beat of the wind
And the song of your strings
Knowing that you can let go
Because there is another
Who is holding tight
And taking care

Fly across the seasons of time
Float on the summer breeze
And ride out the winter storm
Surf on the autumn currents
And climb the summer thermals
But when the air is still and calm
Return to me and rest easy
Gather your strength

So that you will be ready
Ready to rise again

Be my kite:
Fly high and swoop low
Kiss the veil of the clouds
And taste the salty ocean spray
Wink knowingly at the birds
And giggle at the startled butterflies
Be my eyes beyond the horizon
And my ears upon the breeze
Then come home and tell me all
All the secrets of the spheres

So let the wind tussle your hair
But not tangle your mind
For there is no direction without intent
And be sure to let the sun warm your face
But not melt your will
For there is no freedom without choice
And now be my kite

Fly for me
Fly to me
Fly!

A Good Book

Nothing looks so innocent
And yet is so complicit
Nothing seems so ordinary
And yet is so extraordinary
Nothing appears so similar
And yet is so diverse
As a good book

Words cannot express
The power of a good book
The dizzy swirling galaxies
That can hide between two plain covers
The heart-twisting dramas
That can unwind along a trail of letters
The fizz-bubbling mirth
That can break ranks from the march of
     pages

Nothing is so publicly sold
And yet so privately consumed

Nothing seems so plentiful

And yet is so rare

Nothing appears so contained

And yet is so infinite

As a good book

Animated Life

Sometimes it seems that you're not
      listening,

But I know that you can hear the birdsong
      in the forest

And the harrowing, anguished cry of a
      mother's loss.

I know that the breathless sounds of
      passion reach you

And that lonely sighs of despair fill your
      ears.

I know that you are listening,

Because I am listening too

And we cannot but be moved

By the soundtrack of life.

Sometimes it seems that you're not seeing,

But I know that you can see beauty
      through the artist's eye

And ugliness in the cancer of rampant,
      selfish greed.

I know that the sight of carefree children
      reach you

And that poverty's wasteland blots your
vision.

I know that you are seeing,

Because I am seeing too

And we cannot but be enrapt

By the canvass of life.

Sometimes it seems that you're not
speaking,

But I know that you recount the tales of
everyday heroes

And gossip about the vampires that suck
society dry.

I know that words of poetry swirl in your
mouth

And that shouts of abuse spill from your
lips.

I know that you are speaking,

Because I am speaking too

And we cannot but be enchanted

By the story of life.

Sometimes it seems that you're not
breathing,

But I know that you can smell the sweet
  perfume of flowers

And the stench of rotten lies, like
  decomposing carcasses.

I know that the aroma of love intoxicates
  you

And the stink of hatred reaches your
  nostrils.

I know that you are breathing,

Because I am breathing too

And we cannot but be infused

With the scent of life.

Sometimes it seems that you're not feeling,

But I know that your sky lights up with
  firework jubilation

And you languish sometimes in
  depression's dark valley.

I know that the sloshing tide of
  contentment has lapped your shores

And the sludge of self-deprecation has
  mired your path.

I know that you are feeling,

Because I am feeling too

And we cannot but be bubbling
With the emotion of life.

Kingdom of Magic

Sacred world of fairies and elves,
Angels of light, and weavers of spells,
Friends of the earth, of the sky and the sea,
Charming our hopes, alive in our dreams

Perhaps one day, when we truly believe,
We'll awake from our slumber, and there
  you will be:
A kingdom of magic and wonder and gleam,
Larger than life; dream of our dreams.

Rivers Run Deep

No rhymes to part my waiting lips
No words to tease my fingertips
My muse has gone on walkabout
When did the storm become a drought?

No brush to paint the empty space
No pen to sketch the smiling face
My world is grey with black and white
What happened to the coloured light?

And yet I know that beauty's face
Can never fade without a trace
And dreams are conjured in our sleep
For rivers that inspire run deep.

Happy Days

These are happy days
Blissful days
Days of peace and contentment
Of morning walks along the river
And evening calls of smoky silk

These are happy days
Wishful days
Days of dreams and possibilities
Of young love in the bud of spring
And a writer's life unfurling

I know it was not always so
These days of birds and squirrels
But at least for today
(And today is enough)
These are happy days

These are happy days
Artful days

Days of painting and poetry
Of tracing the contours of beauty
And learning to be playful again

These are happy days
Drifting days
Days of freedom and discovery
Of travelling to new and exotic lands
And seeing home with new eyes

I know that I share with another
These days of texting and kisses
So at least through the winter
(And now spring is here)
These are happy days

These are happy days
Braided days
Days of comfort and intimacy
Of weaving the threads of family
And starting a brand new tapestry

These are happy days
Sunshine days
Days of writing and reflecting
Of reaching for the heights of lofty spires
And flowing in the slipstream of
        synchronised rowers

I know they will not last
These days of smiles and sighing
But at least for now
(And now is all there is)
These are happy days.

The Writer

I write my waking incoherence
And when I sleep, I dream in words;
I write out lines as daily penance
And let them go, like captive birds.

The words are seeded in the darkness,
Plucked like stars from midnight skies;
I may not know their rhyme or reason,
Or if they're foolish, foul or wise.

I write in ink on crushed papyrus,
I write in blood to spread the virus;
I write for love, I write for money,
I write in vinegar and honey.

The joy is in the puzzle making,
In finding pieces that might fit;
It's not unlike the art of baking,
Or solving riddles bit by bit.

I write in pictograms and stone,
I write with feathers and with bone;
I write for fame, I write for history,
I write in code and silent mystery.

The pain is in the shards of meaning
Piercing into mental flesh;
It's not unlike the knife of healing
Cleaning out a wound that's fresh.

I write in tones that cast a spell,
I write in heaven and in hell;
I write alive, I write when dormant,
I write in tune and script discordant.

The words are borrowed, begged and stolen,
Yet these words are mine to give;
The belly of my words are swollen
And given birth, they start to live.

I write my muddled hero's journey
And when I fall, words pick me up;

I write out sentences that turn me,
Questing, towards the gilded cup.

I write to breathe, I write to survive,
I write to believe, I write to strive;
I write to conceive, I write to thrive,
It's writing that keeps me alert and alive.

Never

Though pressure builds and workload piles
Never forfeit joys nor smiles
Never lose your hold on hope
You have the means and you will cope
Never lose your will to win
Have confidence in strength within
And know that as you persevere
What you strive for will draw near.

Poets Must Be

If it is poets you seek

Tarry not beside the well-kept literary
    graves

Of those whose time and place is past

Poets must be in that time

When change upsets the veneer of order

When confusion threatens to overwhelm

When the air is pregnant with revolution

Poets must be in that place

Where language of the heart is being
    purged

Where voices of dissent are being silenced

Where words of inspiration give life to dying
    souls

If it is poets you seek

Stray into the entangled expressive
    wilderness

Of those whose time and place is now.

Treasure Hunt

Each day I set out,
Like a curious scout,
In search of a land of surprises;
And the treasures I find,
In the earth and my mind,
Are like beauty in all its disguises.

There's the scent of the rain
And a church window pane,
The kiss of my love and her smile;
There's the dog's wagging tail
And a card in the mail,
The shard of a bright coloured tile.

By the end of the day,
Spent at work or at play,
I add to the chest of my treasures:
The plume of a bird,
A song that I heard –
I'm rich with my horde of small pleasures.

Stripped

Stripped of all the trappings, the clatter;
Bare without the wrappings, the chatter.
So much of me remains untouched,
    unseen;
So many worlds are still unfound that
    matter.

The way an unexpected music swell
Can sweep me, tumbling, in a frothy bliss;
Or how a skilfully crafted spell
Of words enchants as much as any kiss.

Unplugged, the silence is brimming with
    sound;
Unlocked, the horizon need know no
    bound.
So much to re-imagine, to re-dream;
So many universes spinning round.

The way tangled roots in a forest patch
Can reconnect me to life's web, and tug

At my senses, giving me space to catch
My breath and feel revived by nature's hug.

Unseen, the flames of quiet passion
    burning;
Unheard, the cogs of creation turning;
Untold, the lament of a heart's yearning;
Stripped bare, the journey of a soul's
    learning.

Wings

I leap from the land to shin the skies
To climb the clouds and chase sunrise
I dance over cotton wool fields of delight
And dive in the ocean of sensory flight

The whine and the drone
The pitch and the tone
A shining bird sings
A mind spreads its wings.

Vukani! Wake Up!

There was a time when I was passionate:
    seizing the day
    discovering new worlds
    searching for meaning
    challenging my beliefs
    making a difference

Now the passion has turned to indifference:
    pressured by work
    drained by committees
    tied by obligations
    weighed by responsibilities
    tired by expectations

Vukani! Wake up!
life is passing by -
it is time
to give up spectator status
and become a player again.

That Big Thing

I've given up waiting
For that big thing
That will change everything:
The big break
That will launch a dream career
The big adventure
That will script a hero's journey
The big idea
That will carve a notch in history

The thing is that bigger
Is not only not always better
It's also not always what it seems:
Some big things (like coral reefs)
Are really small things made big
Some small things (like embryos)
Are really big things made small
Still other big things (like celebrities)
Are big at small things, but small at big
        things

So now I'm much more interested
In the small things
That are probably the essence of all things:
The scientist fathoms a big universe
By delving into its smallest parts
The merchant grows a big business
By doing myriad small things well
The artist paints a big dream
One small brushstroke at a time.

Walking in the Air

Oh, the places I've been
The things I've seen
With you, it's true:
From London lights to opera flights
And orange crescent moons
From apple walks to bedroom talks
And bright un-birthday tunes

Oh, the mountains I've crossed
The fears I've lost
With you, I flew:
From setting suns to dancing drums
And whirling dervish flair
From rhyming streams to snowman dreams
And walking on the air

Oh, the journeys we'll take
The home we'll make
With you, life's new:
From rocking trains to picture frames
And ventures of the mind
From battles won to family fun
And destinies entwined.

Walk On

When the life you know is shattered
And you're left wounded by the blast
When everything that once was whole
Is scattered in broken pieces
Walk on

When pain is tearing you apart
And yet you cannot shed a tear
When people talk in whispered tones
And all you want to do is scream
Walk on

When the ground gives way beneath you
And you're swept out to the ocean
When chaos swirls like tempest clouds
And the rain is unrelenting
Walk on

When you're cheated on and lied to
By the one who said they loved you

When the kiss you thought was tender
Leaves a bitter trace of poison
Walk on

When your inner world has frozen
Yet the world outside keeps turning
When the sun still shines and friends laugh
Yet all you feel is dark and sad
Walk on

When the one you shared your life with
Is taken from your warm embrace
When all that's left is a dull ache
And the icy hand of sorrow
Walk on

When you're duty bound and shackled
And there's no way out of the maze
When obligations weigh you down
And expectations tie you up
Walk on

When you're running life on empty
And exhausting all your reserves
When all you want to do is sleep
Or curl up in a ball and hide
Walk on

When each morning begs a reason
For why you should get up at all
When each evening brings a shadow
Of haunted dreams and memories
Walk on

When goals can no longer inspire
And hopes are tainted with despair
When anywhere seems much too far
And your biggest wish is just to stop
Walk on.

Bee-lieve

As you nurture new buds and fresh shoots
Don't let cruel words strangle each blossom
Rather pluck them right out by their roots
And be happy to tangle and toss 'em
Yes, just leave them behind
(They're like weeds in your mind)
And believe in yourself –
Bee-lieve.

What the buzz are they bumbling about?
What the fuzz are they mumbling about?
They're just grumbling and fumbling
And stumbling about;
Their thoughts have no power
Their words have no clout
So believe in yourself –
No doubt.

As you stretch out your wings wide and
      roam

Through new days that are dark or are
 sunny

You're expanding the reach of your home

And besides that, you're making sweet
 honey

Yes, I think you will find

You're the best of your kind

So believe in yourself –

Bee-lieve.

What the chit are they chattering about?

What the flit are they nattering about?

They're just clattering and battering

And scattering about;

Their looks have no poison

Their deeds turn about

So believe in yourself –

No doubt.

As you fly by from flowers to trees

And you feel that the strain may be
 showing

Just remember, you're surfing the breeze

There's no telling the places you're going
You're the dance of new rhymes
You're the song of our times
So believe in yourself –
Bee-lieve.

Chronic Rhyme Disease (CRD)

I swear I will not bow to rhyme
(this time)
For I must learn to let words flow
(let go)
And not to drum with sonic beat
(like feet)
Or try to net the perfect match
(to catch)

But now I see I've failed once more
(my flaw)
To scatter words like falling leaves
(from trees)
Instead like hiccups in my chest
(no rest)
I search for words that sound the same
(this game)

They call it Chronic Rhyme Disease
(don't tease!)

Or CRD in doctor-speak
(I'm weak!)
The illness isn't hard to spot
(it's not!)
And leaves the victim quite distraught
(in short)

I guess I'm one such hapless bard
(it's hard)
Still trapped within a cage of words
(like birds)
A lover of the lilt of lines
(like chimes)
An addict of the rhyming mode
(this ode).

Dreaming of my Muse

We met beneath the veil of night,
'Cross time and space, to re-unite,
Like friends of old, like karmic mates,
To exchange dreams, and recall fates

Then into the ocean, an island our goal,
Refreshing our bodies and cleansing our
souls,
And finally to stand in naked embrace,
A vision of beauty, a moment of grace

On waking once more to the bright light of
day,
The shimmering mirage of my dream fades
away,
And I'm left with a memory, a few precious
clues,
Of the glorious meeting between me and my
muse.

Linger Longer

Hearken back to days of yore
Before the rule of less-is-more
When love and loss, for worse or better
Whispered secrets in a letter

Reminisce on ages past
Before the curse of clocks was cast
When language still could linger longer
And poets' words were potions stronger

Cast a longing backward glance
Before science started its advance
When mystic spells and invocations
Sealed the fate of kings and nations

Recollect ancestral fires
Before bound books captured desires
When lifeblood flowed in stories told
And myths recalled wise words of old

Forget these not nor tarry long
Before Time's tide, words carry on
When language-drops look sure to drown
Fear not, for more will soon rain down.

New Boots

I bought new boots today
Where they will take me no one can say
It will be a new place
That leaves behind with hardly a trace
A landscape now past
And a love never destined to last.

So I'm travelling light now
A few memories is all I'll allow
The future lies ahead
A new path beckons for me to tread
And with these new boots on
I'm headed straight for the horizon.

No-Doo-Bee-Days

Doo-bee, doo-bee, doo-bee, doo-ways –
You've just gotta love them no-doo-bee
days.
No grind and no sweat; no work set to do,
Nobody to please; nobody but you.

Do nothing on benches of sun-dappled
shade,
Do nothing in cafes with fresh lemonade.
On beds and on sofas, with books and TV –
No-do days are dandy; what's more, they
are free.

No cook and no clean; no list of to-dos,
No drop and no fetch; no guilt in a snooze.
Doo-bee, doo-bee, doo-bee, doo-ways –
You've just gotta love them no-doo-bee
days.

I Want to Be A Writer

'I want to be a writer, Mom
Is there a secret trick?'

'The trick, my girl, is just to write
To write through thin and thick.'

'But what if I get writer's block
What if the page stays empty?'

'Then write about what's in your head
You'll find that there is plenty'

'But what if it's not good enough
And rambles like a letter?'

'What's *good* is in the reader's eye
Besides, you'll just get better'

'I want to be a writer, Mom
But my friends might not agree'

'When you wake up and want to write
A writer you will be'.

Chasing the Blue

We're chasing after blue
In skies of white and grey
The gap where sun bursts through
To brighten stormy days

We're shooting for the blue
Beyond the green and brown
When earthly strides won't do
To take us where we're bound

We're dreaming of the blue
Where oceans ebb and flow
Our aim and flight is true
Like arrows from the bow

We're reaching for the blue
Ahead of humdrum days
We're powered by the hue
Of shining azure ways

We're chasing after blue
And shall not rest or tire
Together we'll get through
And quench our blue desire.

This Is Your Time

This is your time
Your time to rise
To blaze and shine
Don't say 'too late'
Don't wait for fate
To knock your door
Just take the floor
Take centre stage
Break out the cage
And act your dreams
Dream your story
Once-upon-a-time is now
The page is blank
You have the how
This is your time
Rewrite your rhyme
And take a bow

This is your time
Your time to lead

To show the way

To seize the day

Don't stay a moment

Longer looking back

Your track is straight ahead

You tread the warrior's path

Don't fear, attack

Take giant leaps

Across the void

Into the great unknown

You've grown, now reap

What you have sown

This is your time

Let brass bells chime

The past has flown

This is your time

Your time to live

To love and laugh

To trust your inner guide

Take pride in what

You've done and what

You've yet to do, to be
You'll see that life is not
All strife and pain
The rain is only passing by
So why not sing and splash
And flash your sound
Your brilliance, resilience
In turning things around
This is your time
To rise and shine
You're skyward bound.

Box Life

We live our life in boxes
Proclaiming: 'I'm not free!'
The strangest paradox is
Each box was built by me

Somehow, a box is cosy
A box keeps strangers out
Protects us from the nosey
And leaves no room for doubt

We live our life in boxes
Complaining: 'I can't see!'
And yet the paradox is
That others can't see me

But still, a box is tidy
A box clears up the mess
Brings order and sobriety
Declutters hoards of stress

We live our life in boxes
Until we step outside
The funny thing with locks is
The keys are in our mind

So take that box and blow it
Sky high – you'll love the view!
Your life's not square, so show it:
The curve, the kink, the skew

We box our life from living
Until we knock walls down
The shape of life is giving
And boxed-up Jack's a clown

I'm getting out, I'm letting go
Who dreams big, boxed inside?
The swirling dance of life must flow
So burst your box and join the tide

Escape

When the clocks
Have all stopped
When you're stuck
Out of luck
Waiting and weary
For something to happen ...

You'll know that the show
Can go on
With crazy dreams
And incredible schemes
Freshly invented
To shatter the frozen rhyme
Of time

When you're bored
In a box
When you're trapped
Tightly wrapped

Wishing and wanting
To make your escape ...

You'll find that the mind
Can burst free
Into dazzling vistas
And remarkable twisters
Newly discovered
To explode the prison case
Of space.

Setting Oil, Rising Sol

The tide is rising
Carbonosaurs roar, defiant
Before vanishing
In a puff of black smoke

The smog is setting
Photopreneurs hatch, hungry
Before flourishing
In a field of white light.

The Urgency of Now

This day, this year, this life
Let me live
In the exquisite urgency of Now

Grant me the strength to let go
Of the past
For the past is a ghostly shroud
That can haunt my nights
And cloud my days
Distracting from the urgency of Now

Grant me the wisdom to let go
Of the future
For the future is a diaphanous dream
That can transfix my gaze
And disorient my feet
Diverting from the urgency of Now

Grant me the will to wake up
To the truth

That Now is all there really is

That the greatest gift of all

To myself and to others

Is to be present in the urgency of Now

As for the who, the what, the where

And the why

As for the answers to the eternal questions

That are born of Now

And demand a reply

Let these give me wings in the urgency of
Now

As for the road, the rhyme, the reason

Of my time

As for the highs, the lows, the journey

That marks my passage

And fades to dust

Let these be for love in the urgency of Now

As for the pain, the loss, the dark

Of this life

As for the joy, the gain, the light

That gives me courage

And feeds my hope

Let these steel my faith in the urgency of
Now

This life, this year, this day

Let me love

In the eternal urgency of Now.

Wordspell

Turning over the leaf,
You peer underneath,
Perhaps in search of a clue
As to why, on this day,
And why, in this way,
I'm writing a letter to you.

Well, that's a good question,
Which I'll try to answer
By telling it straight and true.
You see, since I was eight
(So maybe it's fate)
This writing is just what I do.

It seems strange to say it,
But in life, as I play it,
Words have helped me get through.
They help me unravel
The road that I travel;
The mysteries of where, why and who.

It's the writing that moulds,

As the story unfolds,

New lessons to bite off and chew.

There is power in words

That we choose to concoct

In a magical alphabet brew.

Now, I'm no magician,

But I've a strong intuition

That words cast a spell on you too.

Success

Success.
It's not about where you were born
Or the colour of your face
It's not about who your parents are
Or where you secured a place

Success is about how far you can travel
And how much you can learn
How your roots can become shoots
And your bitter seasons can turn

Success.
It's not about how high you have risen
Or how much you've got stashed
It's not about how widely you're known
Or with whom you've been flashed

Success is about how deep you can care
And how hard you can try

How your nights can become lights
And your crazy ideas can fly

Success.
It's not about how clever you are
Or how ruthless you can be
It's not about what plaudits you've won
Or your monuments to greed

Success is about how well you can do
With the hand you've been given
How your heart can become strong
With the love that you're living.

Revolution

There's talk of revolution
In the markets and the streets
There's talk of love and hatred
In the rhyme of hip-hop beats

They say a change is coming
To the corridors of power
They say the day of judgement
Draws nearer by the hour

There's news of revolution
In the papers and the wires
There's news of greed and hunger
And it's spreading like wild fires

They say the planet's burning
From our love affair with stuff
They say we're suicidal
For not knowing what's enough

Let's start the revolution
For the migrants and the slaves
Let's start regeneration
With the sun and wind and waves

They say the world awakens
As the networks spark and grow
They say the future brightens
As we share the things we know

Let's join the revolution
At the factories and the farms
Let's join the call to action
Syncing hearts and linking arms

They say an Age is dawning
As the prophecies unwind
For the biggest revolution
Is a metamorphic mind

So be the revolution
For the ninety-nine per cent

Be the change you want to see
And make your chosen dent.

One of a Kind

On this day, stop a while ... and think
Years lie ahead and you stand on the brink
Hopes and dreams and fears as well
What will be only time will tell
But, wherever life takes you, bear this
thought in mind
You're unique, you're special, you're one of
a kind.

A New Light is Born

Looking around, it sometimes seems so
hopeless

Violence and war, suffering and more, each
way that you turn

Yet is it not true that life is for the learning

And from the depths of darkness, a new
light is born

If only we'd see all the love amidst the
chaos

People who care, joys that we share, peace
that abounds,

Then we would know, in truth it's not so
hopeless

Each time we love another, a new light is
born

It's time to break free from the rhetoric of
doomsday

If we understand our life is in our hands,
it's up to us

We shape our world, it's us who makes the
     difference

If we change the world gets better and a
     new light is born.

The Candle That Burns

As we walk the path of life, at times it is
hard

To keep ourselves from losing hope and
remember who we are

But there's a light in our hearts and we
never walk alone

The candle that burns guides us through
the great unknown

We listen to the daily news of hunger, war
and strife

We wonder what it's leading to, is this all
there is to life?

But then from deep down within, there's a
flicker of light

The candle that burns is the love which
makes things right

So be brave and be bold, hold your head up
high

Shine your light, don't ever give up, those
who succeed are those who try

And then your life can be a light to help
others along the way

The candle that burns is the promise of
dawning day

The candle that burns is the spirit within

Let it burn day and night, do not let it grow
dim

Do not hide it away, let its beauty shine
through

The candle that burns is the best in me and
you.

Threads of Culture

Across space and time, like a delicate web
On the large loom of life, with a silver-like
thread
Is woven a garment for people to wear -
It's the clothing of culture, the spirit we
share.

Spinnings of music, weavings of dance
Stitches of history, patterns of chance
Fusions of fibre, mixtures of trait
Clashes of colour, designings of fate

Joining the past and the future to be
Through stories and rituals and visions and
dreams
Forming knots of tradition and braidings of
blood -
This cultural tapestry is the life that we
love.

Seed of Thought

When you discover a seed of thought
Take care to gently sow it
Water with imagination
It'll sprout before you know it
Fertilise with deep reflection
The rays of insight will grow it
As you nurture your inner garden
You will blossom as a poet.

Promise Me

Promise me you'll not forget anything we've
shared

Promise me that you'll reach out even when
you're scared

Promise me you'll not regret anything
you've said

Promise me that you'll learn from every
path we tread

Promise me you'll not give up until you're
flying free

Promise me that you'll explore wondrous
worlds with me

Promise me you'll not forsake your faith in
Neverland

Promise me you'll dream of us walking
hand in hand

Promise me you'll not destroy fragile bonds
of trust

Promise me you'll always speak the honest
truth you must

Promise me you'll not believe in stereotypes
 that scar

Promise me that you'll perceive how
 beautiful you are

Promise me you'll not desert the passion of
 love's way

Promise that you'll fly with me forever come
 what may

Promise me all of these things, but be
 always aware

My biggest fear remains that I will damage
 what is rare.

Sanctuary

I came to this place, alone and confused
My true love shattered, my trust abused

Dream catchers and dragonflies
Bird feathers and butterflies

I came to this place, bruised and bleeding
And was welcomed into a home of healing

Bright crystals and pixie folk
Aroma candles and incense smoke

I came to this place, and found respite
A sister's care, a nephew's delight

Forest walks and playful hours
Lush green plants and cheerful flowers

I came to this place, exiled refugee
And discovered here a sanctuary.

Feather Signs

The sign of a feather
Reveals when, not whether
We will be together
Through all kinds of weather
In worlds here and nether
In soul love forever.

Golden Thread

Hanging by a golden thread
Between the living and the dead
Between beginning and the end
Between a soul mate and a friend

Choosing not to sever ties
In the midst of near goodbyes
In the midst of stepping back
In the midst of changing track

Weaving strands into a rope
Across the gulf of damaged hope
Across the stream of misled fears
Across the space of future years.

Darkness and Light

When the sun set on my blazing love
And my sky was awash with blood
You were the first star on the horizon
You were the sliver moon of dim hope

When the dark snuffed out my tiny flame
And my world was plunged into black
You were the faint glow of the Milky Way
You were the luminescent moon of waxing
    faith

And when the night ends as it surely must
And my life is reborn to the day
You will be the warm rays of the new dawn
You will be the bright light of love's zenith.

Far Away

While we're apart – each night and day –
Just close your eyes and softly say:
"There's no such place as far away".

I Still Believe In Us

I still believe in us
Not in what we were
But what we are
Not in what we could have been
But what we can be

I still believe in us
Not in fanciful dreams
But tough reality
Not in promises of ever after
But here and now

I still believe in us
Not in discarding the past
But remembering it clearly
Not in guessing the future
But creating it daily.

The Bookshop

I waited
I was there
Searching the faces
There in the bookshop
But she did not come today
I know because I looked for her
Expecting to recognise her
Any moment to find her
But it was not to be
Maybe next time
But not today
Not today

I wonder
Could it be
She was waylaid –
Missed the train or bus
Bumped into an old friend
Went back to check on the stove
Was she running a little late

Did she arrive after I left
I guess it could happen
So maybe next week
Just not today
Not today

I wonder
If she waited too
If she looked for me
And thought I didn't come
That I somehow got the date wrong
Did she sigh over her latte and books
And search among mystery faces
Wishing Neruda's poetry to life
Until the realisation dawned
That time is out of sync
And it's not today
It's not today

We met
Just the once
And now I wonder

If she even remembers the time
The night she visited in my dream
The way we saw each other and knew
Knew that we had come home
And I woke with an aching
With a deep sad longing
To find her once again
So why not today?
Why not today?

Of course
I will return
And I will wait
And I will keep looking
Among the pages and words
Searching for her beautiful face
In the bookshop of our destiny
Calling out her silent name
Imagining our meeting
Even if not today
Then very soon
If not today.

Who Lives There?

I wonder who lives there
In the flat over the common
With the window with the flowers
And the lamp and the sparkling butterfly?
What do they think when they look out
And see the world traipsing by
And watch the dogs running
And the leaves falling?

I wonder what they dream
As they gaze across to the river
With the longboats with the chimneys
And the swans and the enigmatic names?
Who do they pine for as they look out
And marvel at the ever changing sky
And sense the moods shifting
And the light fading?

I wonder if they see me
Walking past along the path
With my jacket with the colours
And my hat and my crazy imaginings?
Do they ever notice when I look up
And reach inside their cosy world
And touch them with curiosity
And a strange longing?

Brush Strokes

Fragrant flower blooms
In the cracks of grey pavement crowds –
A passing intoxication

Luminous flare bursts
In the swell of black cinema skies –
An accidental touch

Mesmeric song ripples
In the glass of reflective train ponds –
A siren glance

Exotic spice floats
On the lips of swirling cocktail seas –
An innocent kiss

Butterfly caress flits
Across the page of white daydream script –
A love fantasy.

Book of Lovers

Upon these pages
Dreams take flight
The words of sages
Shine their light

Seasons turn
Feelings churn
Passions burn
Spirits learn

Between these covers
Seeds take hold
The fields of lovers
Turn to gold.

What If?

What if the home that you've been making
And the smile that you've been faking
Have left you lost in space
Feeling anything but free?

Will you let go of the past
To reveal your fate at last
And will you rise to meet the tide
To restore your inner pride?

What if the bread that you've been breaking
And the hands that you've been shaking
Have brought you face to face
With your own worst enemy?

Will you open up your mind
To accept the worlds you find?
And will you let yourself forgive
To restore your zest to live?

What if the dream that you've been shaping
And the path that you've been taking
Have brought you to a place
That is neither land nor sea?

Will you find it in your heart
To make a fresh new start?
And will you stretch your very soul
To reach that higher goal?

One Mad Moment

One stray spark of wild imagining
Of "alive with possibility" and "what if"
One cheeky taunt of self-daring
Of "what the hell" and "why not"
One decisive click of mental resolve
Of "you only live once" and "just do it"

One endless day of expectation
Of pep-talks and reassurance
One pulsing hour of preparation
Of feet-binding and stomach-knotting
One insane shuffle to the edge
With clinging toes and jelly legs

One crazy countdown to nothingness
Five, four, three, two, one, BUNGI!
One mad moment of wingless flight
Of swan-dive perfection and aerial elegance
One scream-choked spike of frozen panic
Of free-fall plummeting and certain death

One crashing wave of frothing relief

Of elastic grace and bouncing back

One fiery explosion of exhilaration

Of head-spinning blood-pumping ecstasy

One virgin sacrifice who lived to tell the tale

Of escaping the jaws of the wild Zambezi.

Feeling Small

When I'm feeling sad and small
I curl up in a little ball
And wish the watching world away
I close my eyes and quietly say:
No one knows and no one cares
And I am no one after all

When I'm feeling just so-so
I cast adrift and let it flow
And watch the tide within the bay
I look across the waves and say:
Someone sees and someone shares
And I am someone in the know

When I'm feeling top and tall
I spread my arms to welcome all
And greet each brand new dawning day
I lift my eyes and boldly say:
One who soars is one who dares
And I am one and I am all.

Let Them

Let them rip and tear our pages
They cannot mute our story
Let them smash and break our pictures
They cannot kill our smiles

For our words have power
And our joy is like a rock
Our tale is star enchanted
And our happiness is an ocean

Let them swear and curse our fates
They cannot change our destiny
Let them pierce and pry our safety
They cannot intimidate our dreams

For our bond is of the moon
And our weapons made of light
Our art inspires creation
And all that's good is on our side

Let them taunt and mock our morals
They cannot shake our conscience
Let them deny and decry our love
They are but passing strangers

For our inner voice is clear
And our actions speak more true
Our roots of love are strong
And our wings of trust are sure.

Life in Pieces

I. Paradise

My life was full
Crammed and spammed and jammed
Full of stuff and puff
Beyond enough
There were people to meet
Faces to greet
Hands to shake
Deals to make
No time to take a break
From the busyness of it all
The deadlines and budgets
The headlines and fudge-its
And that's not even counting
The mounting expectations
And ladder climbing
To great destinations
Until the day
It all gave way

II. Disquiet

My life was full
A trumpeting horn of plenty
But gently
The cracks appeared
And what I feared
Came creeping
Seeping
Through the floors, the doors
And every gap in my crowded days
A shrouded haze of discontent
Malevolent
In silent ways
Sowing seeds of destruction
Growing weeds of corruption
Like the gnawing rust of years
And the clawing dust in gears
Like trickling sand
That's how it began

III. Descent

My life was full
Then in a flash it crashed
And I was dashed
On rocks of shame
My ego smashed
By waves of blame
Nothing would ever be the same
I clutched at straws
And heard them snap
I ran through doors
Into a trap
A maze of dead-end rescue plans
A band of thieves and rival clans
I fled
I bled
And every thread I grabbed
Unravelled only more
Of what my life had been before

IV. Disintegration

My life was in pieces
Shattered and splattered
And scattered to the winds
Of indifference
Amazed, I gazed around and saw
Shards of love
Unspoken
Now broken
Stunned and numbed, I kicked
A fragment of work
Once polished
Now demolished
I did not have the heart
To start
To pick them up
Those pieces of me
Torn apart
So I just let them be

V. Despair

My life was empty

Weary

Dreary

Eerie

With shadows shifting, demons drifting

Yelling in my head:

I should be dead!

What's the point? Just look around

Not a sound

Not a soul

None to console

No goal

No get-up-and-go

No flow

On life's stage, this page

Is stained and torn

Time to get out of town

Time to bring my curtain down

VI. Desperation

My life was empty
My hand and the gun were one
My finger, the trigger
The barrel seemed bigger
From close up
Everything else was far away
All the things I'd done
The battles won
The hollow acclaim
The pride in my name
My faraway life with my faraway wife
These were things from a distant land
And a living past
Now fading fast
Now, close to hand
A squeeze on the gun
Then the sun
Broke through

VII. Redemption

My life was empty
It needed to be, for me to see
What life is worth
What can give birth through me
If I open up to a greater force
That invisible source
That fires the heart and inspires the mind
That quickens the spirit
And whispers 'just do it!'
I've started again
Rebuilding my bridges
With paintbrush and pen
With family and friends
It's more about people, less about reasons
Less about busy, more about seasons
Less about doing, more about knowing
My life is full
But not overflowing.

Twinkering (Vb, P Pr)

Making changes, swift and small
That seem to matter not at all
Yet send us forth on tangled ways
Into the heart of life's great maze.

Free Falling

Over the edge
At World's End
And Adventure's Beginning

Free
Falling
Unfixed and unnerved
With emotions jangled and raw
Past ties tangled
Taught and stretching
Fraught and frightening
Swan-diving into my fear
Cloud-riding

Free
Falling
Towards the promise
The hope
Of a New World
The scope to explore

To learn
To burn the fire of knowing
To feel the tug of growing

Free
Falling
Throwing the rope
That reaches across
Weaving the bridge
That breaches beyond
The restless ruthless tide
Of need amidst plenty
And want that is empty

Free
Falling
Straining to hear
My calling
My bliss
Somewhere in the mist

Over the edge

At World's End

And Adventure's Beginning.

Wasted Days

So many wasted days
I scarcely dare to count them
Turgid, tempestuous days
That muddied life's pure fountain

So many restless nights
Ticking through each hour
Inane, insomniac nights
When sweet sleep turned to sour

So many futile ways
They stack up like a mountain
Dead-end, diversionary ways
I scarcely dare to count them

So many false bright lights
Each beacon and each tower
Manic, magnificent lights
Ticking down each hour.

Feel

It's not what you do –
Not the mop on the floor
Or the plaque on your door
Not the pat on your back
Or the plaudits you lack –
It's how what you do
Makes you feel
How you feel

It's not what you say –
Not the tone of your voice
Or the words of your choice
Not the wisdom you spout
Or the anger let out –
It's how what you say
Makes me feel
What I feel

It's not what you wear –
Not the latest new fashion

Or the colour of passion
Not the shades of the season
Or the fad beyond reason –
It's how what you wear
Makes you feel
How you feel

It's not where you go –
Not the oceans you sail
Or the summits you scale
Not the lands that you reach
Or the chasms you breach –
It's how where you go
Makes you feel
What you feel

It's not what you think –
Not the bright new ideas
Or the futures you fear
Not the voice in your head
Or the dreams left unsaid –
It's how what you think

Makes you feel
How you feel

It's not what you believe –
Not the scripture you read
Or the faith that you lead
Not the god that you name
Or the sins that you shame –
It's how what you believe
Makes you feel
What you feel

It's not what you give –
Not the money or time
Or the things left behind
Not the temples of gold
Or the stories you've told –
It's how what you give
Makes us feel
How we feel

It's not how you love –
Not the roses and cards
Or the prose from the bards
Not the stars and the moon
Or the lyrical tune –
It's how all your love
Makes me feel
What I feel.

You and Me, Here and Now

What if it's now?
That fateful moment
When everything turns
Silent, invisible gears shifting
And suddenly, your life, or mine
Changes forever
Sets off on a different trajectory
Enters a steep climb
Or stalls into a precipitous dive

What if this very instant
This magic moment
Is now?

What if it's here?
That special place
Where destiny seeds
Dark, patient forces incubating
And suddenly, your future, or mine
Changes forever

Marks a new point of departure
Lays a fresh foundation
Or connects to roots long buried

What if this very location
This pivotal place
Is here?

What if it's me?
That reluctant hero
Who hears the call
Tepid, timid heart beating
And suddenly, your quest, or mine
Changes forever
Looms larger in the lens of days
Stretches to the curved horizon
Or plumbs the depth of ocean

What if this ordinary soul
This unexpected hero
Is me?

What if it's you?

That elusive lover

Who fits my edges

Yin and yang forces swirling

And suddenly, your dream, or mine

Changes forever

Refracts through a new prism

Bends to someone else's bow

Or reaches for another's star

What if this missing half

This integral lover

Is you?

Making Ripples

I am streaming words into the void
A pointless, poignant pulsing of mind
Seeking nothing and finding it
Among mute stars winking

I am broadcasting signals into the noise
A futile, fulfilling flashing of ideas
Lighting caverns and fizzling out
Among deaf bats clicking

I am whispering secrets into the matrix
A confounding, complex coding of heart
Turning keyholes and tumbling locks
Among blind alleys echoing

I am dripping odes into the ocean
A silly, sublime splashing of meaning
Making ripples and merging back
Among thought currents flowing.